LESSER LETHAL
OPTIONS

By Timothy Hightshoe

Includes:
Basic Use of Force
Basic Tactical Baton
Defense Sprays
Handcuffing & Searching Techniques
(Part of the Security Officers Training Series)

INTRODUCTION

Each of the booklets in the Security Officer's Training Series is based on the Use of Force Model (UFM) developed by Dr. Franklin Graves and Professor Gregory J. Conner of the University of Illinois Police Training Center, and used at the Federal Law Enforcement Training Center (FLETC). The concepts used throughout these booklets are a compilation of many individuals' work and not wholly original ideas of my own. I have compiled many of the techniques used by Local and Federal Law Enforcement Agency's into what I hope is an easy to understand system; one which allows the Security Officer to work within the confines of the law. This particular booklet and the subsequent ones are based primarily on Colorado Revised Statutes (CRS). As a security officer you should familiarize yourself with the specific laws that apply to your state and municipality. It is the individual's responsibility to keep current on changes to the laws affecting their job.

These booklets are intended to provide the security officer with the basic information needed to complete their duty assignments.

Timothy Hightshoe

USE OF FORCE

DEFINITIONS

Before we can begin a discussion on the use of force, we must first develop a common vocabulary. In this section we will define the most commonly used terms in the UFM as currently defined by Colorado Revised Statutes, again you need to be familiar with the specifics of your location. By understanding the legal meanings of the terms listed here you will be better able to understand the UFM. In addition, a thorough understanding of these terms will aid you in applying the proper "Balanced Force" in the performance of your duties.

BODILY INJURY: Physical pain, illness, or any impairment of physical or mental condition.

DEADLY PHYSICAL FORCE: "Deadly force," is defined as intentional use of force, which can cause death or serious bodily injury or which creates a degree of risk that a reasonable and prudent person would consider likely to cause death or serious bodily injury. It includes, but is not limited to, use of firearms, neck restraint, and intentional intervention with a vehicle (forcible stops or ramming).

DEADLY WEAPON: Any of the following, which in the manner it is used or intended to be used is capable of producing death or serious bodily injury: (I) a firearm, whether loaded or unloaded; (II) a knife; (III) a bludgeon: or (IV) any other weapon, device, instrument, material, or substance, whether animate or inanimate.

DE-ESCALATE: To use the least amount of force to stop the action of a subject and reduce the amount of force applied as the threat is neutralized or becomes compliant.

DUTY TO REPORT USE OF FORCE BY SECURITY OFFICERS: A Security Officer who, in pursuance of such officer's security duties, witnesses another Security Officer, in pursuance of such other Security Officer's security duties in carrying out an arrest of any person, placing any person under detention, taking any person into custody, or in the process of crowd control, use physical force,

[1]

which exceeds the degree of physical force permitted pursuant to section 18-1-704 C.R.S. must report such use of force to such officer's immediate supervisor.

The above paragraph reflects the statute as written for the state of Colorado, however almost all states have similar statutes in place for security and law enforcement officers.

ELECTRONIC IMMOBILIZING DEVICE: (EID) A lesser lethal, conducted energy weapon, that uses propelled wires or direct contact, to conduct electronic energy to a remote target, thereby controlling and overriding the central nervous system of the body.

JEOPARDY: A hazard, a threat, or a peril.

IMMEDIATE THREAT: An immediate threat is considered to exist if the suspect has demonstrated actions that would lead one to reasonably believe they will continue to pose a threat of death or serious bodily injury if not apprehended without delay.

IMMINENT DANGER: Any action which leads an officer to reasonably believe a suspect's actions would lead to the loss of human life, including the officer's own life. Or any action, which places a person in immediate threat of serious physical injury.

LETHAL WEAPON: Any object or material, when in the manner it is used or intended to be used, is capable of producing death or serious bodily injury.

LESSER LETHAL WEAPON: Any object or material, when in the manner it is used or intended to be used, is not likely to result in death or serious bodily injury. Any weapon, even those classified as lesser lethal can be lethal if used improperly or in an inappropriate or unapproved manner. As conditions unknown to the security officer (i.e.: heart conditions, asthma, allergies, drug or alcohol overdose) may also affect a subject resulting in death even with the appropriate use of a less than lethal weapon, the term "less than lethal" was an earlier term and is still used in many areas when referring to this type of weapon..

PHYSICAL OR NON-DEADLY FORCE: Any force, action, or weapon, which produces a result that is necessary to control the actions of another and does not involve the use of deadly physical force.

REASONABLE BELIEF: Having knowledge of facts, which, although not amounting to direct knowledge, would cause a reasonable person, knowing the same facts, to reasonably conclude the same thing.

SERIOUS BODILY INJURY: Bodily injury, which, either at the time of the actual injury or at a later time, involves a substantial risk of death, a substantial risk of serious permanent disfigurement, a substantial risk of protracted loss or impairment of the function of any part or organ of the body, or breaks, fractures, or burns of the second or third degree.

USE OF EXCESSIVE FORCE: (1) Subject to the provisions of section 18-1-704 C.R.S., a Security Officer who uses excessive force in the pursuance of such officer's security duties shall be subject to the criminal laws of this state to the same degree as any other citizen, including the provisions of part 1 of article 3 of this title concerning homicide and related offenses and the provisions of part 2 of said article 3 concerning assaults. (2) As used in this section, "excessive force" means physical force, which exceeds the degree of physical force permitted pursuant to section 18-1-704. The use of excessive force shall be presumed when a Security Officer continues to apply physical force in excess of the force permitted by section 18-1-704 to a person who has been rendered incapable of resisting arrest.

Again the above paragraph reflects the statute as it is written under Colorado Revised Statutes. Make sure you are fully aware of the pertinent statute for the state and municipality where you are working.

USE OF FORCE MODEL (UFM)

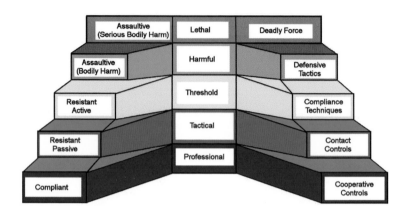

The primary concern in the use of force is to use only the **MINIMUM** force needed to accomplish the task. Officers engaged in security duties must use only that force which is reasonably necessary in accordance with applicable laws.

The UFM is designed to assist the officer in identifying and interpreting the right level of force to use in performance of their duties.

The elements involved in the use of force are visually presented via the Totality Triangle. Each of these elements make-up the three section, five-tier, color enhanced structure of the Use of Force Model (UFM). Each component of the triangle: subject action, risk perception and officer response are essential for a balanced use of force.

Totality Triangle

Risk Perception: The situations that are perceived by the "reasonable officer" within a confrontational environment, which present a risk or potential risk to the officer's safety. Issues including the severity of the crime, degree of subject non-compliance, knowledge of the subject's previous actions, etc., can act as a test for reasonableness and for placement in one or more of the perception categories of the UFM.

Subject Action: The action(s) perceived by the "reasonable officer" that place the subject in one or more of the models compliant/non-compliant categories.

Officer Response: The "balanced" response the reasonable officer could and/or would select from the UFM's identified categories, in order to maintain or regain subject compliance and control.

The proper perception of risk is the core consideration in the decision-making process toward proper force utilization. It is the functional foundation for the two other major model categories and integral to their understanding and application.

The UFM is designed to assist the security officer in identifying and interpreting the right level of force to use in performance of their duties. Color is used in the UFM to enhance understanding of the categories. Research has shown a relationship between the five basic colors and levels of action or alertness. Each color has the following description:

Blue - is the lowest level on the UFM. This level of perception includes the day-to-day non-threatening type activities. Most encounters at this level involve the use of verbal skills with compliant actors.

Green - is the level where there is usually additional actor behavior, which categorizes the person as a passive resistor who may require an increase in verbal or physical response from the officer.

Yellow - signals a need for increased alertness due to a recognized threat from the active resister. A variety of compliance techniques may be used to gain compliance from this person.

Orange - denotes an assessment of imminent bodily harm to you or someone else. You should direct your energy and tactics toward self-defense or threat elimination.

Red - indicates the highest level of threat. Imminent serious bodily harm or death to you or someone else has been assessed. Survival skills and aggressive action to stop the threat is required.

RISK PERCEPTION CATEGORIES

Professional Perception

Professional perception (Blue) is the baseline of the pyramid. Each day when you begin your shift, you must recognize and remain aware of the risks you could face. These risks include threats to your personal safety that come from people you make contact with and/or the environment in which you work. The potential of risk could be during a routine building check, or a chance encounter on the property you are watching. The assessment of risk must begin at this level and never fall below this baseline during your shift.

Tactical Perception

Tactical perception (Green) is employed when you sense an increased threat and specific safety strategies are deployed. These should include a call for backup and not approaching or contacting the subject until that backup arrives.

Threshold Perception

Threshold perception (Yellow) is an increased alertness due to perception of a threat and a recognized danger. Many times this level represents the critical intervention phase of a confrontation, since a tactical plan must be developed to insure officer safety. This advanced degree of risk potential should motivate the officer to increase the level of attention away from the subject and more directly toward the actions of the subject or others present.

Harmful Perception

Harmful perception (Orange) denotes an assessment of danger to you or others. You must recognize the increased likelihood of injury to you, and must direct your energy and tactics towards defense and the safety of all present.

Lethal Threat Perception

Lethal threat perception (RED) is the highest level and indicates the highest threat to you or others. This potentially lethal level is the most infrequent and the most crucial for you to recognize and act on. You must maintain the highest-level of awareness and be prepared to use survival skills.

SUBJECT ACTION CATEGORIES

Compliant

This is the lowest level of actor on the UFM. The vast majority of security encounters involve cooperative complaint actors who respond to verbal requests and directions. The likelihood of a physical confrontation is minimal.

Resistant (Passive)

In some contacts, the actor may offer an initial level of confrontation. The actor's resistance is primarily passive, with the actor showing no signs of wanting a physical confrontation.

Resistant (Active)

This is the level where the actor becomes more active in their resistance. The actor will direct his or her physical strength and energy in achieving and or maintaining their resistance.

Assaultive (Bodily Harm)

You recognize active, hostile resistance. There is a reasonable threat of attack to you or someone else. It is a reasonable assumption that the actions of the attacker would not result in serious bodily harm or death.

Assaultive (Serious Bodily Harm/Death)

This is the least encountered, but most serious category. Here you recognize a reasonable threat of serious bodily harm or death to you or another as a result of an attack.

OFFICER RESPONSE CATEGORY

Cooperative Controls

This includes the fundamentals of professional training and the use of a variety of controls including: communication skills, common tactics, body language, etc. The following are tools used at this level:

Mental Preparation: Perception Skills, Risk Assessment Skills, and Survival Orientation.

Spatial Positioning: Office Stance (Interview Stance), Body Language, and Relative Positioning (Reactionary Gap).

Verbal Controls: Communication Skills, Behavioral Assessment.

Contact Controls

In this first instance of non-compliance, the officer must deploy tactical talents to gain control and cooperation through "hands on" techniques designed primarily to guide or direct the subject. The primary force component at this level could be transitional tactics or non-pain compliance techniques.

Those from cooperative controls
Verbal manipulation techniques
Wrist, elbow, and hand position (come alongs) (joint locks)

Compliance Techniques

Tactical procedures at this level now must address the non-compliant subject who has begun to use physical or mechanical energy to enhance non-compliance, while remaining increasingly vigilant for more aggressive behavior from subject. At this stage, the force forms could include: elements of pain compliance, chemical irritants, joint restraints, etc.

Those from cooperative controls and contact controls
Neuromuscular controls
Chemical irritant application
ASP®/Baton in a non-striking mode

Defensive Tactics

At this stage the resistant actor becomes directly assaultive toward you or another. You are justified in taking appropriate steps to immediately cease the assaultive actions and to gain compliance and maintain control of the actor once compliance is achieved.

All controls from lower categories
Escape Techniques: For use in escape from grabs and chokes
Assault Defense: To include the use of head, hands, elbows, feet, and knees, in warding off or countering the subject assault
Impact Tools: Used to fend off or gain control of subject. Blocks, strikes, and jabs to **non-lethal areas** would be justified.
Weapons retention is a must at this level

Deadly Force

The officer is now confronted with an assaultive situation that reaches the ultimate degree of danger. Absolute and immediate tactics must be deployed to stop the lethal threat and secure conclusive compliance and control.

All tools are available at this level to include firearms, lethal strikes with ASP®/Baton, or any object at hand

FORCE CONTINUUM

Level 1 - Officer Presence:

Sublevels = Standing, Walking, Running

Compliant subjects are those individuals who offer no verbal or physical resistance to the officer's commands and demonstrate their cooperation by immediately responding to directions.

Level 2 - Verbal Commands

Sublevels = Whisper, Conversation, Shout

Passive resistant subjects are those individuals who refuse to comply with commands but are not attempting to physically prevent or defeat the officer's commands or contact controls. If the actor does not present a physical threat to you or someone else at this level call for local Law Enforcement to enforce compliance.

Level 3 - Control and Restraint

Sublevels = Empty Hands, Restraints, OC Spray

Active resistant subjects are those individuals who refuse to comply with the officer's commands and are physically resisting an officer's control techniques, or individuals whose combination of words and actions may present a physical threat to others. This is the first level where security officers may use physical force. Physical force at this level should be dedicated to defense only; force should not be used to create compliance. Call for back up and Law Enforcement.

Level 4 - Impact Tools:

Sublevels = ASP batons, Wood Batons, Flashlights

Active resistant subjects are those individuals who refuse to comply with the officer's commands and are physically resisting an officer's control techniques, or individuals whose actions present a physical threat to others. Force at this level is designed to reduce the actor's ability to inflict injury to yourself or others. Use loud repeated verbal commands, and only the physical force needed to accomplish the goal of threat reduction. Call for Law Enforcement back up. Follow the instructions of police as they arrive on scene.

Level 5- Temporary Incapacitation:

Sublevels = Empty Hands, OC Spray, Impact Tools

Combative subjects are those individuals who attempt to defeat an officer's compliance techniques in that they are resistant, combative and overtly attempting to overpower the officer. This is one of the most dangerous situations, the actor may be trying to disarm you and cause physical injury. Use all available techniques to gain distance. If possible, put an obstacle (car, fence, table, etc) between you and the actor. Call for Law Enforcement, and additional backup. Remember to use loud repeated verbal commands during the encounter, and use only the minimum force necessary to ensure control of the situation.

Level 6 - Deadly Force:

Sublevels = Empty Hands, OC Spray, Impact Tools, Firearms
(Warning shots are not allowed)

Deadly force assaults are any assaults where the officer has reason to believe the individual's actions are likely to cause death or serious bodily injury. This is the worst-case situation we can find ourselves in, and we must stay vigilant to this possibility though it will be the least used level in the continuum. At this level, situations will present themselves very rapidly or without warning. It is critical to act quickly to stop the threat before deadly force can be used against you or someone else. Remember the actor makes the decision that you must use deadly force against him by his actions. After the use of a firearm, move to cover, if you haven't, call for Law Enforcement and remain on guard as the actor may still be a threat or someone else may become involved. If the situation is secure, try to holster your weapon before Law Enforcement arrives. Keep in mind, that when Law Enforcement arrives, they will not immediately know who are the "good guys" and who are the "bad guys". Follow their directions without hesitation—particularly if you have not had the opportunity to holster your weapon by that time.

USE OF FORCE SELF TEST

1. The totality triangle shows what type of force should be used?

A.   True
B.   False

2. "Serious Bodily Injury" is defined as "Physical pain, illness, or any impairment of the physical or mental condition?

A.   True
B.   False

3. At Use of Force Continuum Level 2 you may employ verbal commands and OC spray on a subject who refuses to leave your site?

A.   True
B.   False

4. The color blue on the UFM is the lowest level on the model and includes day-to-day non-threatening type activities?

A.   True
B.   False

5. The primary concern in the use of force is to use as much force as you can to stop a threat before it become a threat?

A.   True
B.   False

6. Risk Perception can be formed from the severity of the crime, degree of subject noncompliance, knowledge of subject's previous actions, etc. However, it must be based on the "reasonable officer's" standard?

A.   True
B.   False

7. A Deadly Weapon is defined as any weapon intended to cause death or serious bodily injury, to include a knife, bludgeon, and a loaded firearm.

A. True
B. False

8. If confronted with a deadly assault, you may not use a baton or OC to stop the attack?

A. True
B. False

9. If a person is offering only verbal resistance, you may spray them with OC to gain compliance with your instructions?

A. True
B. False

10. Your presence, in uniform, is not considered a Use of Force?

A. True
B. False

11. Physical or Non-Deadly Force is any force, action, or weapon, which produces a result that is necessary to control the actions of another and does not involve the use of deadly physical force?

A. True
B. False

12. You must always use the minimum amount of force needed to accomplish the task?

A. True
B. False

13. Before you use a firearm on an attacker, you must fire at least one warning shot?

A.   True
B.   False

14. An officer may use a baton on a person who has in the past attacked an officer, but is currently complying with instructions as this prevents injury to the officer?

A.   True
B.   False

15. All a subject must demonstrate is his intent and capability to cause serious bodily injury to you or another before you may use deadly force against him?

A.   True
B.   False

16. If faced with a deadly force assault, you must respond with deadly force to prevent a lawsuit?

A.   True
B.   False

17. You must start at level one of the Use of Force Continuum and move up from there?

A.   True
B.   False

18. Your uniform will identify you as a "good guy" to all law enforcement officers as they arrive at the location of an assault?

A.   True
B.   False

19. One reason for Use of Force training and education is to help prevent or reduce lawsuits against you and your company?

A.   True
B.   False

20. Once you have used deadly force, you cannot use a lesser level of force?

A.   True
B.   False

TACTICAL BATON

WARNINGS AND SAFETY

Before we begin the study of tactical batons, a few words about safety.

In this booklet we will be discussing the tactical use of the baton as well as describing training drills. If you are in close proximity to others extreme caution must be used at all times when practicing. No horseplay should be tolerated in the practice area. It is the individual's responsibility to ensure the area is clear prior to deploying their baton. Any time you are using the baton; eye protection should be used. Some of the exercises may be better accomplished with the use of training batons; these are padded batons that can be used with moderate force to practice proper technique. Anytime a training baton is used against a person, the person being struck should use padding, a mouth guard and eye protection -- at all times.

This booklet is designed to give the student the basic information to develop the skills to use a baton in the performance of their duties. We will also discuss the proper application of force in accordance with Colorado Revised Statutes. If you live outside of the State of Colorado, you should be familiar with your state's laws and act in accordance with them.

Though the baton is primarily used in a lesser lethal role, it can be a deadly weapon. Therefore, it is important you have a thorough understanding of the strike zones and where they fall on the UFM. A thorough understanding of the application of force with a baton can help reduce or eliminate criminal and civil liabilities. While the primary focus of this booklet will be the ASP® style baton, many of the techniques used for the ASP® transfer well to other batons.

TYPES OF BATONS

Straight Baton: This is essentially a straight wooden stick, which is one of the oldest weapons known to man. It has been around since the caveman with little to no changes. Though there are many martial arts that teach stick fighting, we will only be covering the security use of this weapon. As with all batons, it is primarily a defensive weapon capable of blocking and striking an aggressive subject. There are several advantages, including speed and a few additional jab type strikes. However, the straight baton has fallen out of favor with most security and law enforcement officers: the primary reason being its lack of convenience. The straight baton can also be a hassle to carry, especially when getting in and out of a vehicle. In addition, because of its size it can be slow to deploy.

ASP® Baton: This is a brand name of baton that has become synonymous with collapsible batons. There are a host of cheap copies of the ASP®, which you can pick up at most gun shows for as little as $20.00. The problem with many of these copycats is the quality of steel they are made from. Some may look good, but will bend when used. Others do not lock open properly or will stick open requiring excessive force to close. It is recommended you purchase an ASP® or other quality collapsible baton. Monadnock® is a relative newcomer on the market, but is a good quality product. One advantage to the Monadnock® baton is that it uses an internal locking system, which allows the baton to be collapsed by pushing a button on the tail cap of the baton and pressing the baton closed. This has proven to be a reliable system with few malfunctions. The primary advantage to the ASP® style baton is convenience; it can be carried without hanging up on seatbelts or other items in the environment you are working in. An additional advantage to this style of baton is psychological; the mere act of deploying the baton may de-escalate a developing situation without having to apply physical force.

Flashlights: This is one of the most misunderstood tools you carry; many officers do not realize how devastating a weapon this can be. Some officers carry a large flashlight, but do not think to consider using it as an impact weapon. The 4, 5 or 6 D cell Mag Lights® can cause considerable damage and should be treated just like a baton.

One of the major advantages to carrying a large flashlight is its dual purpose. In an attempt to limit the amount of equipment on a duty belt, consider removing the baton and carrying a larger style flashlight. You should have a flashlight on your belt anyway. While the larger flashlight has the same disadvantages as a straight baton, it offers some significant advantages in searching and as a visual deterrent. In addition to its use as an impact weapon and in searching, a very bright light can be used to temporarily blind or disorient a subject. This type of use is classified at a lower level on the UFM, but still allows you to have an impact weapon in your hand if the subject becomes assaultive.

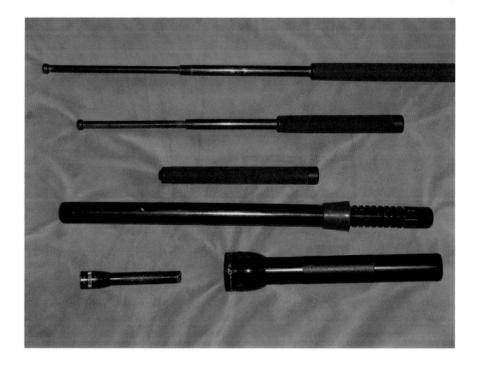

CARRY POSITIONS AND CARRIERS

There are so many types of carriers on the market today it would be impossible to cover all types, so just a few notes on them.

First: Buy a quality carrier/holster sized to fit your baton.

Second: For the collapsible baton, find one that will allow an open baton to be holstered.

Third: Ensure the carrier has sufficient retention to prevent loss of the weapon while running or fighting.

Lastly: Make sure you can effectively deploy the baton from whatever carrier you have chosen.

There are two basic carries for the baton, first is the weapon side (strong side) carry, which offers many advantages; of which weapon retention may be the most important. In addition to retention, this carry puts the baton immediately available to your strong hand, which reduces the time it takes to deploy it in an emergency. Another advantage to this type of carry; you do not have to reach across your body to deploy the weapon, which reduces the chance of having your arms pinned to your body and not being able to defend yourself.

Some considerations to carrying the baton on the weapon side are: type and size of your baton, and size of your body. Another consideration to think about is where you wear the baton on the duty belt. Some officers prefer to carry it in front of their firearm, while others place it behind the weapon. The type of baton can be also be a factor in determining placement. However, keep in mind that how you shoot from retention can become a serious issue. The latter is a much bigger problem than some officers

realize. I have seen batons shot on the firing range when carried in front of the weapon. Before carrying in this configuration practice retention drills with an **UNLOADED** firearm to see if your technique will pose a potential risk.

The second position is the retention side (weak side) carry; this is the preferred carry for the straight baton due to the ease of draw, which is its primary advantage. However, this carry is not recommended for the collapsible baton because of weapon retention issues. Additionally it requires a cross body draw that puts you at a disadvantage in close quarters.

Another consideration to the way you carry your baton, if you carry a collapsible baton, is how to put the baton in your carrier. Again there are two basic schools of thought and we will address both, but the most important concept is to carry it the same way every time.

First: Let's look at carrying the baton tip or shaft up, this allows you to rapidly grip the baton for the closed mode, in addition to rapid deployment in closed mode it prevents the baton from opening in the holster if you have one that will allow an open baton to be holstered (recommended). The only disadvantage I see to this carry is in rapid deployment for weapon strikes in the open mode. The tip up carry places your hand in an awkward position during deployment and opening of the baton. For some officers, this is not a problem and again consistency is more important.

Second: The baton tip or shaft down method of carry. This is my preferred carry. This allows you to grip the baton and deploy it forcefully, the amount of psychological impact this can have is impressive. I have de-escalated possible confrontations by just deploying the baton (**CAUTION**: Use only In Accordance With State and Local Statutes and Company / Department policy) the mere presence of the baton can sometimes convince noncompliant subjects to cooperate. However, you should never draw or deploy your baton as a bluff. Anytime it leaves the holster you should be prepared to use it properly.

The other advantage to this position is in replacing the baton; it is the same position for an open or closed baton. If you have used your baton to stop a threat and you need to go hands on, one of the best places for the baton is back in the holster -- **NEVER** leave an uncontrolled weapon in the environment. With a good holster, one that allows an open baton to be holstered, simply return it to the holster without closing.

Important considerations in carrying a baton: Deployment, Retention, and Convenience. Remember, a baton left behind can't save your life.

Open Asp ® Baton returned to holster

AUTHORIZED BATON USE

The baton can be a very effective tool for the security officer. Even though it can be used at different levels of the UFM, it is important to note that the first time you can use the baton under the UFM is at level three, where a subject becomes actively resistant. At this level of resistance, force should only be used in a defensive role. The baton will primarily be used in the non-striking mode; generally this will be the closed mode. For security officers ensuring compliance with directions is not a primary concern. If a person refuses to leave a site or property, call for Law Enforcement to enforce compliance. The main concern for security officers needs to be the safety of themselves and the others they are assigned to protect. You must realize every fight you find yourself in contains a deadly weapon—YOURS.

Level four of the UFM is the first time you are justified in using a baton in a striking mode. At this point, the subject has become a threat to you or someone else and you must **STOP** the threat. Use only those strikes needed to **STOP** the threat. Remember, just because someone has pushed you to this action, you are not permitted to get even. This sounds simple, but in a fight emotions become involved and judgment can be clouded. As in most use of force cases, you will have very little time to decide how much force to use. Keep in mind your actions will be looked at by a lot of other people who have all the time in the world -- after the fact. "Monday Morning Quarterbacks" will tell you in many instances, you used too much or too little force. Follow your training and use only the force you feel necessary at the time. However, anytime a strike is justified, hit as hard as you can. Just as with deadly force you cannot be justified in a half strike. Though this issue may be a little difficult to understand, the difference between a closed, non-striking use of a baton and a full out baton hit are the actions of the subject. Refer to the Use of Force Model for further information on type and justification for baton use.

BATON NOMENCLATURE

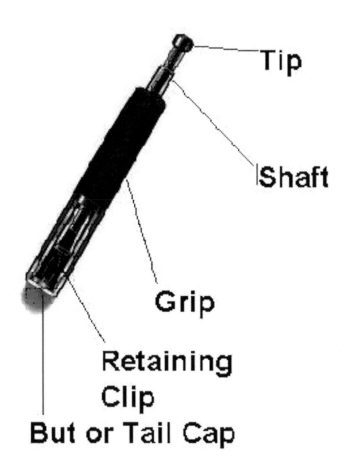

Tip

Shaft

Grip

Retaining
Clip

But or Tail Cap

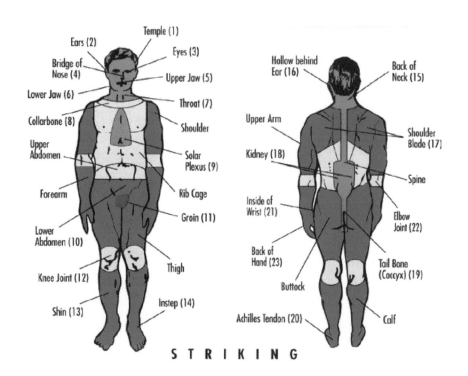

Temple (1)
Ears (2)
Eyes (3)
Bridge of Nose (4)
Upper Jaw (5)
Lower Jaw (6)
Throat (7)
Collarbone (8)
Shoulder
Upper Abdomen
Solar Plexus (9)
Forearm
Rib Cage
Groin (11)
Lower Abdomen (10)
Thigh
Knee Joint (12)
Instep (14)
Shin (13)

Hollow behind Ear (16)
Back of Neck (15)
Upper Arm
Shoulder Blade (17)
Kidney (18)
Spine
Inside of Wrist (21)
Elbow Joint (22)
Back of Hand (23)
Tail Bone (Coccyx) (19)
Buttock
Achilles Tendon (20)
Calf

S T R I K I N G

TARGET AREAS

As you can see on the target chart there are three colors used to help you understand where to strike. Let's look at what each color means.

Green: This indicates the primary target zones on the body. These areas provide the least possibility of serious injury to the subject. These areas can be struck in level 3, 4, or 5 of the UFM. Remember for a strike in level 3 it must be in defense only.

Yellow: These areas pose a substantial risk of injury and should be avoided if possible. Strike these areas only if immediate threat elimination is justified by the subject actions.

Red: This is the highest level of force that can be applied with a baton. This is **LETHAL FORCE.** If you are justified to strike a red zone you are also justified to shoot the subject. Extreme caution must be used in any strike near a red zone.

BATON STRIKES

Though there are several types of strikes; we will talk about two modes: "open" and "closed", as well as three types of strikes: "weapons", "reaction", and "straight" strikes.

Closed Mode Strikes: These strikes are designed primarily to break someone's grip on you or a possible weapon. This mode of strike is usually performed by utilizing the reverse grip with the thumb covering the tip of the baton and striking the hand or other appropriate target (see picture).

Reverse Grip (Closed Mode)

There are three basic strikes:

1) The Weapon's Strike starts from your weapon's (Strong) side and moves cross body.

2) The Reaction Strike starts from your reaction (Weak) side and moves to the weapon side.

3) The Straight Strike is performed by holding the baton in your strong hand and simply punching. This strike is not commonly used in the closed mode and is not considered very effective.

Open Mode Strikes: Are primarily used against an assaultive subject. This mode of strike is usually performed by utilizing a forward grip (see picture).

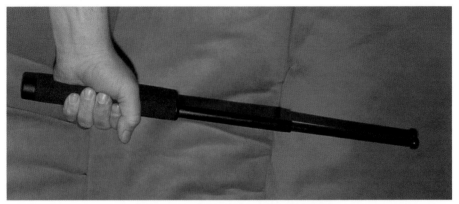

Forward Grip (Open/Striking)

In addition to the three basic strikes of the Closed Mode there are two more strikes that can be performed effectively in the Open Mode. In addition, the Straight Strike, while not considered effective in the Closed Mode is more effective in the Open Mode.

To begin an open mode strike, we must first extend or open the baton. There are three basic methods for opening a tactical baton.

The first method is called "open to the sky". Start by firmly grasping the closed baton in a forward grip and swing rapidly upwards (to the sky) extending and locking the baton open. Caution should be exercised in regard to objects overhead: low ceiling, lights, etc.

The second method is called "open to the ground". Again, firmly grasping the closed baton in a forward grip, swing rapidly down (to the ground) extending and locking the baton open. This is probably the most common opening method. Caution should be exercised in regard to objects or persons near or behind you.

The last method is called a Rapid Weapon's Strike and will be described in more detail later.

1) The Straight Strike is performed by holding the open baton with the strong hand in a forward grip while the weak hand grips the tip end of the shaft in an opposing grip refer to photo. At this point push with both hands. Remember to use an opposing grip. This is used primarily in crowd control situations or to keep a subject back.

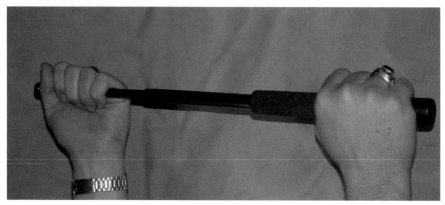

Straight Strike Grip

2) The Rapid Weapon's Strike is done with the baton closed.

Using a forward grip from the closed mode, perform a weapon strike. The swing of the baton will open it during the strike.

3) The Two-Hand Lateral Strike is best described as a baseball swing. Hold the baton as you would a baseball bat and swing. While this type of strike can produce considerable force it also limits your target areas.

There are three basic methods for closing a baton after use:

1) The finger close technique is used primarily in training when the baton has not been forcefully opened. Simply grasp the shaft, twist and close.

2) The tapping method.

This technique is preferred over the combat close in areas where damage may occur from striking the baton against a surface AND when the situation is completely controlled. Hold the extended baton low to the ground and tap the tip several times against the ground, rotating the baton as you do so. Then close the baton utilizing the finger close method.

3) The combat close.

Start by holding the open baton with a reverse grip then strike down forcefully on a hard surface, such as concrete or asphalt. Caution: this method should only be used on solid, hard surfaces as it can damage wood or tile surfaces.

Baton Retention

There are four basic techniques we will mention in this booklet. All of these techniques are performed in the open mode.

1) Twelve to Six: In this technique, grasp the baton with both hands pull up rapidly to the twelve o'clock position, then forcefully push down and back to the six o'clock position.

2) Distract and Cast: Here we pull the baton back over the strong shoulder, then push forward in a casting motion.

3) Air Guitar: For this technique, grasp the baton in the forward grip with the strong hand while the weak hand grabs the shaft of the baton in the middle. Then squat and play an air guitar using your weight to force the baton down.

4) Wrist Turnover: This is a very effective retention technique. Holding the baton in the strong hand, the weak hand grasps the baton shaft just forward the grip. Then rotate the tip of the baton out of the attacker's grip. Remember to rotate towards the thumb of the attacker's hand for this technique to work well. The direction of rotation depends on which hand grabs the baton.

Post-Use Care

As important as it is to use the baton properly, what you do next may be more important. First, be aware that you may have inflicted a large amount of pain and possible injury on the subject. Remain calm and try to calm them. Call 911 for Medical and Police support. Since the subject will be turned over to local Law Enforcement, you must inform them you have stuck the person. Describe as clearly as possible the technique used as well as the location struck. Medical examination is strongly recommended. Document the date, time and name of the officer you informed about the use of your baton. Document what you did as soon as possible, be as descriptive as possible, include number of strikes to which location, type of strike; "Closed weapon strike", "Two-hand lateral strike, etc". Report the use of a baton IAW your company policy.

FINAL THOUGHTS

Just as with any other weapon system, your baton will only be effective if you practice with it. The skills you develop in this or any other course are perishable and need to be practiced often. Refresher courses should be taken on a recurring basis. Caution must be used when practicing the skills you have been shown in this class. Remember the baton can be a deadly weapon and must be used and practiced with, with caution.

IT IS RECOMMENDED YOU PRACTICE THESE SKILLS AND TECHNIQUES REGULARLY

1. Forward Grip
2. Reverse Grip
3. Grip for Straight Strike
4. Open to the Sky
5. Open to the Ground.
6. Finger Close
        Closed Mode Strikes

7. Weapon Strike.
8. Reaction Strike.
Open Strikes

9. Weapon Strike.
10. Reaction Strike.
11. Straight Strike.
12. Two Hand Lateral Strike.
13. Rapid Reaction/Weapon Strike.
14. Combat Close
Retention

15. Distract and Cast
16. 12 to 6
17. Air Guitar
18. Wrist Turnover

TACTICAL BATON SELF TEST

1. The elements involved in the use of force are integrated in the Use of Force Model (UFM) and consist of:

A.   Ability, Opportunity, and Jeopardy
B.   Intent, Capability, and Preclusion
C.   Subject Actions, Risk Perception, and Officer Response
D.   Office Knowledge, Officer Safety, and Office Risk

2. There are five levels in the UFM?

A.   True
B.   False

3. If a subject is actively resisting, without attacking the Security Officer, that officer would be justified in using baton strikes, without further action on the part of the subject?

A.   True
B.   False

4. When are you justified in using baton strikes against a subject?

5. Any cheap baton is good enough for security work?

A.   False
B.   True

6. List the two "modes" of the baton:
    1.
    2.

7. List the Closed mode strikes:

8. List the Open mode strikes:

9. List three ways to open the baton:
     1.
     2.
     3.

10. Officers should avoid striking the subject's head/face, neck/throat, spine, kidneys, groin, and chest as strikes to these areas may produce serious bodily injury or death, or may not be effective in terminating the assaultive actions of the subject.

A.   True
B.   False

11. After striking a subject with a baton, they should be given the opportunity to receive medical attention.

A.   True
B.   False

12. Principal target areas for the baton should included the arms, and legs, though elbows and knees should be avoided.

A.   True
B.   False

13. Where is the best place to carry the baton for retention?

14. There is no need to inform police of a baton strike when they take custody of subject you have struck.

A.   True
B.   False

15. What information should you get from the officer you turn the subject over to after a baton strike?

DEFENSE SPRAYS

WARNINGS AND SAFETY

Since the use of any defense spray, and the conditions of its use are not within the control of DeHLTA instructors, it is the **USER'S OBLIGATION TO DETERMINE CONDITIONS OF SAFE AND EFFECTIVE USE.** DeHLTA instructors are not responsible for inappropriate use. DeHLTA is not responsible for the lack of proper continuing training, or a lack of appropriate policy by any agency using our training guides.

SEVERE IRRITANT: OC is a severe irritant. **AVOID ACCIDENTAL CONTACT WITH EYES, SKIN OR MUCOUS MEMBRANES**: Capsicum-based weapons have immediate and intense effects on the mucous membranes of humans and other mammals.

CHILDREN: Keep out of the reach of children. Defense sprays should not be handled by minors.

CONTENTS ARE UNDER PRESSURE: Do not puncture or incinerate can.

FLAMMABLE: If "FLAMMABLE" is printed on the weapon, the user should not expose the weapon to heat, sparks (including those from electric stun guns and tasers) or flame. Do not store above temperatures listed on weapon. **DO NOT USE A TASER OR ALLOW A TASER TO BE USED ON ANYONE WHO HAS BEEN SPRAYED WITH THIS TYPE WEAPON.**

TESTING AND EVALUATIONS: Users should be properly trained prior to testing or operating any defense spray product.

FIRST USE: Upon receipt of a new or unused device, the user should spray a short burst **OUTDOORS** with the wind at his / her back, away from people and animals. Any units in the field that have not been test-fired should be tested. This ensures all units are operational, and that there has not been any damage during storage, carrying or shipping.

BYSTANDERS: Caution must be used in certain environments, such as **Nursing Homes, Children's Centers, Hospitals** or any facility that uses a central ventilation system. Certain models are not designed for indoor use and spray may travel into the ventilation system, affecting bystanders. If a weapon must be used where bystanders can be affected (including outdoors crowds), the user must remove innocent bystanders from the area prior to application. This can be accomplished by personal contact or loud speakers notifying bystanders and inhabitants that the weapon is going to be used and all individuals should keep their doors and windows closed, turn off air conditioning units, and stay inside buildings or leave the area.

DEADLY FORCE:

DO NOT USE A CAPSICUM-BASED WEAPON AGAINST AN ATTACKER USING A DEADLY WEAPON AGAINST YOU OR SOMEONE ELSE.

In this situation a higher level of force may be appropriate and justified. As with any use of force option, the user should rely heavily on experience and training, and should discontinue the use of force when resistance or aggressive behavior ceases.

TYPES OF DEFENSE SPRAYS

CS: Orthochlorobenzylidenemalononitrile
Agent State: Micro-Particulated Solid
Classification: Lacrimator, Irritant, Sternutator
Chemical: Synthetic
Effect: 3 to 10 Seconds
Produces: Tearing and Lacrimation
Irritation of the skin
No effect on animals
Contamination: Severe problem; will attach to clothes and furnishings
Recovery: 10 Minutes
Side Effects: Dermatitis, allergic reactions, Carcinogen
Shelf life: 3 Years

CN: Cohloroacetophenone
Agent State: Micro-Particulated Solid
Classification: Lacrimator, Irritant
Chemical: Synthetic
Effect: 5 to 10 seconds
Produces: Tearing
Burning sensation on skin
Photophobia (sensitivity to light)
Contamination: Severe problem; will attach to clothes and furnishings
Recovery: Less than 10 Minutes
Side Effects: Documented second degree burns,
Acute "vesicular dermatitis"
Toxic; documented incidents of death
Shelf life: 3 Years

Neither of these products is suitable for use as a personal defense spray. CS is used in crowd control by law enforcement and military, and should not be used for daily carry. Both of the above products can be found mixed with OC. These combination products must be avoided to reduce your liability. With the mixed products you increase the chances of a severe adverse reaction to the spray.

OLEORESIN CAPSICUM

Capsicum: Capsicums are chili peppers, which occur in many varieties ranging from mild to hot. Capsicum encompasses twenty species and some 300 varieties of pepper plants.

Anatomy and Chemical Characteristics of Capsicum: The property that separates the Capsicum family from other plant groups, and the very essence of the chili pepper is an alkaloid called capsaicin (Kaps-sa-i-sin), an unusually powerful and pungent crystalline substance found in no other plant. Capsaicin is a colorless, crystalline, bitter compound present in capsicum. Capsaicin is produced by the glands at the juncture of the placenta and the pod wall. The capsaicin spreads unevenly throughout the inside of the pod and is concentrated mostly in the placental tissue. The seeds are not the source of heat, as commonly believed.

Capsaicinoids: Capsaicin is not a single substance and is found in five different compounds within chili peppers called Capsaicinoids. They are the actual ingredients that cause the burning sensation and inflammation of the mucous membranes. Capsaicinoids are the source of the "hotness" in chili peppers.

Oleoresin Capsicum (OC): "Oleoresin" is the extracted oil of the dried ripe fruits of the capsicums and contains a complex mixture of highly potent organic compounds.

Testing the "Hotness" of Chili Peppers: SHU versus HPLC:
To scientifically measure the amount of capsaicin in a chili pepper, High Pressure Liquid Chromatography (HPLC) equipment is used to obtain an accurate measurement of Capsaicinoids in percentage.
Scoville Heat Unit (SHU) is another test method dating back to the 1930's; it was replaced by HPLC due to its subjective nature. SHU testing is nothing more than "tongue" tasting of the spice by a panel of five individuals. SHU therefore depends on the taste experience of the panel, which is subjective and based on taste sensitivities that vary from person to person.

Oleoresin Capsicum vs. Capsaicinoids: OC concentration represents the amount of OC (oily resin) in a canister, and not its strength. OC is simply the natural oil extracted from the chili pepper and by itself is not the cause of hotness. As discussed earlier, Capsaicinoids are the cause of hotness in chili peppers; this is why some peppers are hotter than others. For example, an OC spray with 5.5% concentration and more Capsaicinoids can be five times hotter and stronger than one with 10% and less Capsaicinoids:

Brand Name	OC Concentration (%)	Capsaicinoids (%)
First Strike	10%	0.18%
Saber	5%	0.67%
Cap-Stun	5.5%	0.92%

PHYSIOLOGICAL EFFECTS

Capsaicinoids at the proper dosage normally will produce an inflammatory effect that causes mucous membranes to swell, causing an immediate closing of the eyes and uncontrollable coughing. In addition, intense burning of the skin is usually experienced. These physiological effects normally prevent or reduce the subject's ability for aggressive action. The effects are immediate but temporary, and will usually resolve in 45 minutes.

Capsaicinoids primarily affect three target areas:

EYES: Causing immediate closing of the eyes.
RESPIRATORY: Uncontrolled coughing
SKIN: Intense burning sensation

PSYCHOLOGICAL EFFECTS

The primary psychological effect of OC spray occurs in a group setting. Once the physiological effects of the OC have incapacitated one subject, the rest of the group normally will disperse without conflict. This is especially true if you are using a fogging type dispenser. In some cases the presence of an OC canister will cause a subject to rethink his or her actions.

PEPPER SPRAY SAFETY

This book cannot comment on the safety of specific brands of OC, only on general OC products. It is the user's responsibility to check on the reliability and safety of the product they choose to carry. All pepper sprays are not safe for use in a law enforcement / security or personal protection environment. There are a variety of aerosol propellants and carrier formulations used within the industry. Some are relatively safe and some are toxic or environmentally unsafe and should not be sprayed directly in the face. For example, Methylene Chloride (synonym: Dichloromenthane), used in some brands, is classified as a carcinogen by the EPA, and can cause permanent tissue damage. There are some sprays with a high Capsaicinoid content (over 1%) that can cause 2nd and 3rd degree burns to skin as well as permanent blindness. This type of product is normally used in animal control (Bear Defense) products, and should not be used against a person.

As of this writing, OC has not been listed as the cause of death in any specific case, but has been linked to at least 22 in-custody deaths (see article published by the International Association of Chiefs of Police entitled: **"Pepper Spray and In-Custody Deaths"** by John Granfield, Jami Onnen and Charles S. Petty, MD). Of these deaths, 18 were caused by positional asphyxia, with drugs and or disease also being listed as contributing factors. In the remaining four cases, three involved a drug (cocaine) related death and one involved a drug (cocaine) disease related death. The review's results indicate OC was not the cause of death in any of these cases. There have been some in-custody deaths that have listed OC as a contributing factor though not the primary cause of death. If interested you can find a large amount of information on in-custody deaths available on the Internet.

SPRAY PATTERNS

There are three primary methods of dispensing OC; the one you choose should fit your application. There are advantages and disadvantages to each.

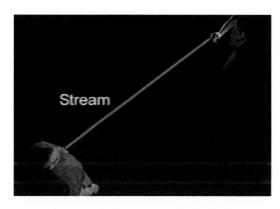

Stream: Stream is considered the best for indoor usage, due to its narrow spray pattern and lower atomization. It is less susceptible to wind movement than the other larger spray patterns. Due to the smaller diameter of the pattern, it requires more precise aiming, and can be blocked by the subject's hand or glasses. Also, due to the smaller pattern, multiple shots may be required to cover the target area.

Foam: Foam has similar characteristics to the Cone & Fog, with the exception that it has minimal effect on the respiratory system and may be used more efficiently indoors. Foam is also messy due to its soapy nature, and can cause unwanted contamination when it gets on clothing, car seats, furniture etc. There is also a potential for gagging and vomiting with foam, as the bubbles enter into the respiratory system during rapid inhalation.

Cone & Fog: These spray patterns atomize and cause a mist in the air, and are more susceptible to wind. Because they are made of smaller airborne droplets they can be inhaled and will therefore affect the respiratory system quicker. They may also enter indoor ventilation systems and effect innocent bystanders.

This type has a large spray pattern and does not require precise aiming. The physiological effects are usually faster due to the smaller droplets immediately depositing on the mucous membranes. In addition, recovery may also be faster.

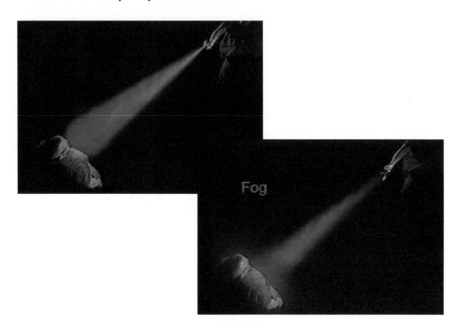

Fog

EFFECTIVE SPRAYING TECHNIQUES

The most effective technique depends on type of spray and environment the spray is deployed in. To simplify the deployment techniques we will assume a stream type canister, and a single subject. Aim the spray directly at the face of the subject (along the eyebrows) from a distance of 5 to 10 feet. Employ a one-second spray with a side-to-side motion. If the subject is still aggressive two to three seconds after initial spray, a second one-second burst should be delivered. Most subjects will automatically close their eyes, as it is a natural reaction, as well as hold their breath when sprayed. If this happens reapply a one-second burst, the capsaicin will attack the mucous membranes of the eyes, causing them to automatically blink, allowing the spray to enter the eyes.

Remember to:

Aim along the eyebrows
Use a one-second burst.
If subject is still aggressive, reapply a one-second burst directly to the eyes.
Avoid Continuous Spraying: Multiple sprays of one-second duration are more effective than a continuous spray.

TARGET PRACTICE

Target practice is as important with defense spray as with a firearm, but is generally overlooked. You must practice the techniques presented in this booklet and continue practicing to remain proficient. It is recommended you purchase inert training canisters, available at most law enforcement supply stores, to practice with. Try to find the same configuration of canister you carry. When practicing, it is best to start in an area with little or no wind and develop your skills. After you have established good marksmanship, practice in varying weather conditions to learn the effect the environment may have on the delivery of the spray. You can visit your local shooting supply store to purchase various targets for use when practicing. It is best to use inert spray to practice with, but you can use active spray. If you are using active spray insure you are not causing contamination of living or working areas. As animals are very susceptible to the effects of OC; also insure you are not contaminating an area with pets or other animals.

IT IS **_NOT_** RECOMMENDED THAT YOU PRACTICE ON FAMILY MEMBERS, FRIENDS OR PETS.

HOLSTER & METHODS OF CARRY

There are three basic methods of carrying and drawing defense sprays.

Pocket or Purse Carry: This method is used more in a personal protection environment than in law enforcement or security. Advantages are availability, concealment and convenience as no additional equipment is required. Disadvantages include: ability to rapidly deploy the defense spray and risk of accidental discharge.

Strong (weapon) Side Carry: The holster is positioned in front of or to the rear of a firearm (if carried). The individual should ensure the spray holster does not interfere with the drawing of the firearm. The device's nozzle should face away from the body (depending on type) and the trigger system should be protected from accidental discharge by the retaining flap. To draw the weapon, the gun or strong hand will reach down and pull up on the holster flap; grasp the canister pulling it up to a ready position, the thumb is not on the trigger (finger on some models) until you are ready to deploy the spray. This technique provides the best aiming and most positive control of the weapon. The disadvantage to this carry is in transitioning to other weapon systems; since the canister is in your strong hand you must re-holster or pass it to your weak hand to utilize a baton, Taser or firearm. Though

this method affords the user the quickest draw, this position is not recommended if you are carrying other weapons (firearm, baton, Taser, etc).

Weak (reaction) Side Carry: The holster is carried on the reaction side with the nozzle pointing away from the body (depending on type). To draw the canister, the weak hand reaches down and pulls up on the holster flap, then grasps the canister. Come up to a ready position; the thumb is not on the trigger (finger on some models) until you are ready to deploy the spray. This is the preferred method of carry as it allows the individual to transition to a baton if the spray is not effective, or if subject elevates the threat. It is important to not have the canister in the weak hand and a firearm in the other as this poses additional dangers. Under high stress, the brain's message (intended for one hand) can go to both hands resulting in an unintentional discharge of your firearm. Do not draw your firearm unless deadly force is justified.

STANCE

Interview Stance: The interview stance is the basic stance for all personal weapons' deployment, and should be used in all unknown risk contacts. This stance is designed to place the individual in a subtle defensive posture.

Position your feet and body at approximately a 45-degree angle, weapon side away from subject. Place your weak (reaction) side leg forward and your strong (weapon) side leg back. You feet should be slightly more than shoulder width apart and your knees slightly bent. Avoid the "funnel" position of standing directly in front of the subject. This position allows the subject to obtain a focal awareness point on you and places you at a disadvantage.

Ready Position: From the interview stance, place the hand you will draw the canister with on the holster and unsnap the flap. This is a preparatory position to be used if the subject has not yet become physically aggressive.

Remember the most effective spraying distance is 5 to 10 feet. This distance allows the OC to work while maintaining a "reactionary gap" between you and the subject.

HANDCUFFING AND RESTRAINTS

For security and law enforcement personnel, after a subject has been sprayed, allow approximately five seconds for the mist to dissipate and then use loud repeated verbal commands to direct the subject into a position where you can safely handcuff them. After the subject has been placed at a disadvantage, re-holster the canister (one-handed). Do not drop the canister as this could damage the canister causing an inadvertent discharge, it also places you at risk of being sprayed by the subject or an accomplice. Do not forcibly handcuff a sprayed subject immediately after spraying. Allow the subject to calm down. It is not recommended that individuals using OC for personal protection carry handcuffs unless they have received specific training in their use and application.

Caution: When OC has been inhaled, the respiratory tract is inflamed, and breathing is restricted. Handcuffing the subject behind the back while placing him/her on his/her stomach may cause positional asphyxia. Positional asphyxia occurs when the body position interferes with respiration. This is more of a concern if the subject is overweight or has a comprised respiratory system. If the subject complains of or appears to be having trouble breathing, set the subject up and closely monitor them. CALL FOR MEDICAL RESPONSE.

First Aid

This section applies to anyone exposed to a defense spray. After the situation is under control, ask all affected parties if they are suffering from any serious medical conditions such as asthma, bronchitis, or emphysema. Look for Medical Alert bracelets or necklaces on the subject. If a condition is suspected or if anyone is having trouble breathing seek immediate medical attention.

SEEK IMMEDIATE MEDICAL ATTENTION BY ACTIVATING THE 911 SYSTEM IF ANY ONE AFFECTED:

LOSES CONSCIOUSNESS
SUDDENLY BECOMES INCOHERENT
STARTS LOOKING VERY SICK
STOPS BREATHING
or
BEGINS TO HYPERVENTILATE

Decontamination

WARNING: To avoid further irritation, avoid touching your eyes, nose, mouth, groin and other sensitive areas until you have washed your hands with cold water as hot water re-activates the agent.

AIR: Normal ventilation will usually remove airborne residue from the environment within 45 minutes.

SPRAY NOZZLE: Wipe the nozzle of the canister with a paper towel after application to make sure there is no buildup or residue to accidentally cause irritation. Properly dispose of the paper towel after use.

BODY: Wash the affected skin areas, including hands, with a non-oil based soap, liquid soap, or liquid detergent designed to cut grease and oil—use cool water not warm.

HAIR: If your hair has been contaminated, you may experience a temporary burning of the face or other sensitive parts of the body when taking a shower. Try to prevent contaminated water from running into the groin. If hair is known to be contaminated wash hair in a sink before taking a shower. Always use cool water, as heat will re-activate the agent.

CLOTHING: For clothing stained with OC, wash separately from other clothing, with detergent as usual. A spoonful of baking soda aids in removing the smell of the pepper spray.

JUSTIFIED USE OF FORCE

Capsicum-based weapons can generally first be used at level 3 of the Use of Force Model. They may be employed before physical hands-on force is used.

OC spray is primarily for the purpose of:

1) Providing instantaneous control of highly aggressive, violent persons.

2) Subduing those under the influence of narcotics or alcohol who are aggressive or violent.

3) Controlling single or multiple persons who are non-compliant.

4) Minimizing physical contact, thereby reducing injury and other risks to all involved persons.

5) Reducing the need to escalate to a higher level of force.

OC can also be used to create a reactionary gap, or to delay an assaultive person until police can arrive.

FINAL THOUGHTS

Just as with any other weapon system, your defense spray will only be effective if you carry it and are proficient with its use. The skills you develop from this book or any other training course are perishable and need to be practiced often. Refresher courses should be taken on a recurring basis. Caution must be used when practicing the skills that have been discussed in this book. Remember the best and safest way to practice with defense sprays is to use an inert canister. This allows you to work on marksmanship without risk of contaminating yourself or others. In addition to marksmanship you should determine the effects of your environment on the spray pattern, and learn to judge the distance to your target, which will help prevent deploying the weapon at a distance that is ineffective.

DEFENSE SPRAYS SELF TEST

1. Capsicums are the name for?

    A. Chili Peppers
    B. Black Peppers
    C. Mustard Seeds
    D. A Brand Name

2. Oleoresin Capsicum is?

    A. Crushed Peppers
    B. Extracted oil of chili peppers
    C. Brand name
    D. Oil of raisin

3. What makes chili peppers hot?

    A. Seeds
    B. Capsaicinoids
    C. The red color of the skin
    D. How small they are

4. Hotness of chili peppers are most accurately measured by?

    A. Scoville Heat Units
    B. Irritant
    C. HPLC
    D. Size of seeds

5. Oleoresin Capsicum in categorized as?

    A. Inflammatory
    B. Irritant
    C. Painful
    D. Devastating

6. Oleoresin Capsicum impacts?

    A. Mucous Membranes
    B. Chest
    C. Wrist
    D. Neck

7. Physiological effects of OC are?

    A. Closing of eyes, nausea and headache
    B. Immediate closing of eyes, burning sensation of skin and coughing
    C. Headache and nausea
    D. Stomach upset and headache

8. Physiological effects of OC usually last?

    A. 1 hours
    B. 45 minutes
    C. 5 minutes
    D. 2 hours

9. In regards to Use of Force, pepper spray should be used?

    A. Between verbal commands and physical engagement
    B. After handcuffing and restraint
    C. After physical engagement
    D. Before verbal commands

10. Pepper spray should be used?

    A. At officer discretion, whether the subject complies or not
    B. On noncompliant subjects
    C. When a subject complies with lawful commands
    D. When subject expresses verbal disagreement

11. Pepper sprays have directly caused the following number of deaths?

    A. 4
    B. 0
    C. 26
    D. 94

12. What spray pattern is recommended for indoor use?

    A. Cone
    B. Stream
    C. Fog
    D. Mist

13. Which spray pattern requires precise aiming?

    A. Cone
    B. Fog
    C. Stream
    D. Foam

14. The best method for carry the holster is?

    A. One the non-gun side
    B. In the back of the duty belt
    C. On the gun side
    D. In a pocket

15. The spray should be targeted at?

    A. The nose
    B. Between the eyebrows
    C. The chin
    D. The neck

16. Immediately after spraying you should?

    A. Disengage and get distance from the subject
    B. Request backup assistance
    C. Begin to interview the subject
    D. Spray the subject again

17. Proper first aid and cleaning of the subject is achieved by?

    Saline Solution
    Water
    Ice Pack
    Facing into the wind

18. During transportation, the officer should?

    A. Hogtie the subject to avoid further aggressive behavior
    B. Position the subject to allow easy and free breathing
    C. Place subject face down
    D. None of the above

HANDCUFFING & SEARCHING TECHNIQUES

HANDCUFFING

The use of force option we use more than any other is handcuffing. Consequently, use of force trainers remind us that proper technique and precautions when cuffing and UN-cuffing a subject is one of our most important officer safety considerations. Notwithstanding those times we're happy just to get the cuffs on at all, that's good advice. But what of the cuffs themselves? Do they make a difference? Are there really differences between all of the different cuffs and cuff types available?

Well…of course! After our radios, cell phones and coffee mugs, our cuffs are probably our most used piece of professional equipment. The design and manufacture of anything that's used that often, and performs as vital a function as handcuffs do, is something we should pay attention to.

Whether you prefer hinged or chained handcuffs, the first thing to be aware of is whether your cuffs meet National Institute of Justice (NIJ) Standard 0307.01. This standard specifies that each handcuff shall be able to withstand a tensile force of 495 pounds of force (lbf) without failure. The tested handcuff shall not open under load, shall not show any sign of permanent distortion or fracture and shall function in a normal manner following the test. The standard also specifies that each handcuff shall withstand 204 lbf/inch against cheek plate separation. Many of the cheaper handcuffs on the market do not meet this standard. Is this important? Consider how strong the last really big guy you arrested or detained was, or consider the superhuman strength of a PCP user. Any officer who has worked the streets for a while knows of a local incident in which someone did, in fact, break their cuffs. So, yes, it's important. And, besides, why gamble with the risk?

Next consider how your cuffs double-lock. Double-locking cuffs once they are on a suspect is an important thing to remember—one that is too often forgotten. Double-locking provides safety for the suspect so the cuffs don't tighten and restrict circulation or create lacerations. More important, they provide safety for the officer in several ways:

1) An unlocked set of cuffs is an invitation to a lawsuit for nerve damage or other more visible injuries.

2) An unlocked set of cuffs can be shimmed open—and too many of the really bad guys know how to do this.

3) Double-locked cuffs are more difficult to pick with a bent paper clip or similar object.

4) You won't be tempted to un-cuff your prisoner to adjust a "too tight" pair of cuffs and thus expose yourself to an assault.

There are two common methods for double-locking handcuffs. Some cuffs use a pushpin mechanism, while Smith & Wesson® cuffs have traditionally incorporated a slot-activated mechanism. Some officers prefer one method, while other officers prefer the other. It doesn't matter which mechanism you prefer or are comfortable with, as long as you remember to double-lock every time!

Another consideration for handcuffs is how comfortable they are for the officer to use. Quality handcuffs are contoured in such a way that holding them in the "loaded" position and applying them is noticeably more comfortable than handcuffs with a more square profile. A little thing, perhaps, but one that affects technique.

Handcuffs are an effective way to control a subject that may become or is already aggressive. The proper application of handcuffs should not put you or the subject at risk of personal injury. As security officers, it is not our primary purpose to apprehend (arrest) criminals, but to protect people and property. However, in the protection of people and property we sometimes do need to apprehend or restrain a subject who poises a danger to themselves or others. If an individual becomes assaultive you may need to restrain them until police arrive. It is important to note handcuffs may be used at level 2 of the UFM. At this level, a passive resister who has expressed a willingness to use force against you or another may be restrained or if you are performing an arrest in accordance with the laws of your state and municipality. Normally, at this level, the subject will summit to handcuffing without the use of physical force. Before handcuffing a subject, ensure you completely understand your company's use of force policy, as well as the applicable laws covering use of force. Just because you have handcuffed a subject, does not mean they are "under arrest". Handcuffs may also be used as a safety measure for the officer and the subject. It is important to remember, that in most states, before you can "arrest" a person, that person must have committed a crime in your presence.

First, let's look at the chain type cuff, which is the standard for most law enforcement and security applications. Though there are several different manufacturers of handcuffs it is recommended you stay with one of the major name brands (Smith & Wesson®, Peerless®, American Handcuff® or Hyatt®), this will help ensure the quality of the cuffs used. Some companies may have a policy that identifies a specific brand of handcuffs, make sure you are complying with that policy. The prime advantage to the chain style cuffs is the flexible positioning of the hands. If you have to struggle with the subject, his / her hands may not be in a good position to get the cuffs on. Disadvantages to the chain cuffs, are that the subject has more possible hand movement, and the chain can be a weak point in the system. In addition, caution must be used in handling a handcuffed subject. When you place your hand on the linking chain, the subject can "smack" the cuffs together causing injury to your hand. The subject may also manage to "wrap" the chain trapping your wrist.

Now, hinged cuffs. This type of cuff offers the officer some significant advantages in controlling a restrained subject. The cuffs do not allow the hands to move as freely as chain linked cuffs do and they provide a positive control point -- the hinged section. The only disadvantage I see to hinged cuffs comes in cuffing a combative subject, as it may be difficult to get the cuff into the proper position.

.

NOMENCLATURE — HANDCUFFS

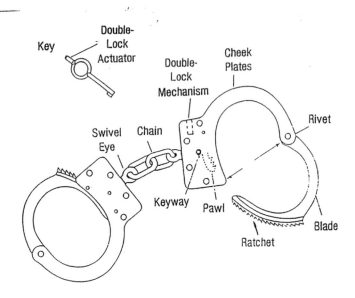

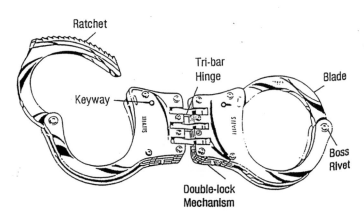

HANDCUFFING PROCEDURES

As security officers, we should not be handcuffing combative subjects very often. Whenever possible do not handcuff a subject without backup. If you are confronted with an overtly hostile situation, **_BACK OFF_**, give yourself a reactionary gap, place an object between you and the combative subject, and call for police and backup. If you or someone else is in imminent danger, use only the force needed to stop the threat. If you are armed with a firearm, draw and order the subject to the ground, arms out, palms up, and facing away from you. This is a final challenge position. Do not approach the subject without backup, and if possible it is best to wait until police arrive. If it is safe, holster your weapon as or before police arrive, remember to:

FOLLOW THE POLICE OFFICER'S INSTRUCTIONS IMMEDIATELY.

Keep in mind the officer responding will not know who the "bad guy" is when he arrives. Your uniform will not give you protection, as they are available through a variety of sources. If the officer orders you to the ground, follow his / her instructions; it's not personal, they are following their department's safety procedures.

If the situation does not allow you to wait for police to arrive, hopefully you will have security backup. In dealing with the situation on your own the following procedures should be followed:

1) Have your backup (over watch) move to a position to the side of the subject, still maintaining a reactionary gap.

2) Have the subject look at the over watch then order them to put their hands in the small of their back, thumbs up and palms out.

3) With your strong hand get your cuffs, grab the chain / hinge, ensure the keyholes are against your palm and the cheek plates are toward you.

4) Move and approach the subject from a different location. This will prevent them from using your voice to get a position on you.

5) Grip the middle two fingers of both of the subject's hands and pull slightly away from the body.

6) Place the blade of the cuff on the hand opposite you at the base of the palm. Between the palm and the wrist is the joint. This area is known as the "valley of the wrist" and is where the handcuffs should be placed. Once in position push down sharply, locking the cuff around the wrist -- do not adjust this cuff yet. Now, pull the other cuff towards the opposite wrist and repeat the same procedure.

7) After both cuffs are locked, adjust them without releasing the chain / hinge. To adjust use your weak hand to close the blade, ratcheting the cuff until it is snug. **Caution**, do not over tighten the cuff. Perform the same steps for the other hand. After both cuffs are adjusted, double-lock and test to ensure the cuffs cannot close further. During cuffing do not release the chain / hinge as this is your positive control point.

The above procedure works well for a subject who was combative and was ordered to the ground. Sometimes we will need to cuff a more compliant subject; in these instances we will handcuff standing:

1) Order the subject to turn around, feet spread, hands in the small of their back thumbs up and palms out.

2) Have the subject lean forward.

3) Follow the same procedures used for the prone cuffing.

Remember to always have backup before handcuffing, if possible. Keep in mind that a compliant subject may become aggressive during handcuffing. Do not discuss whether the person is under arrest with them until after they are cuffed. Be aware of others in the area. During handcuffing, if you are acting as "over watch" you must watch not only the subject, but also everyone in the area. Focus on safety and security for yourself, your partner and the subject to prevent tunnel vision.

After you have handcuffed a subject you are responsible for their safety and welfare. You must take all reasonable actions to prevent injury or unnecessary pain to the subject. You must immediately turn over any person you have in custody to police when they arrive on scene.

SEARCHING

In searching, remember, we are not looking for evidence of crimes, but for weapons. Searches for security officers are a "simple frisk" for weapons. Just as with handcuffing you should never search a subject without backup. A "precautionary check" of the subject should be made before actual searching. Ask the subject if he or she has "any sharp objects or weapons on their person" (i.e. needles, razors, knives, etc.). Security officers are in a high-risk environment for exposure to such health hazards as HIV, hepatitis B and other blood borne pathogens. With that in mind, remember to never reach where you cannot see (i.e. inside pockets, waistbands, etc.). If a bulge is seen, ask the subject what the item is. If a weapon or other contraband if is found, make note of what the item is (white powder, green leafy substance, pistol, etc) and where it came from. When police arrive, turn over any items removed from the subject. Remember you are responsible for anything you have taken from a person.

Some points on a "simple frisk":

1) Again you are not searching for evidentiary purposes -- only for officer safety.

2) Your search should only include a quick pat down of those areas where a weapon could reasonably be believed to be located; such as the upper body, the waistband and the pockets.

3) If at all possible, searches should only be conducted by a person of the same gender. If it is not possible then males should use the back of their hands when searching a female subject.

4) When you check the waistband, do not place your fingers into the waistband, as this could expose you to razors or needles that may be

hidden there. Run your hand along the outside, feeling for possible weapons under the material.

5) Keep all searches professional. A search is not intended to humiliate or embarrass the subject. It is only a safety precaution.

6) If you remove any items from the subject, you are responsible for them. Keep them on your person or secured at all times. If they are turned over to police, instead of the subject, when your involvement is completed; annotate what the item is, a brief description of the item and the name of the officer you turned it over to, along with the date and time in your report.

7) Practice your search technique.

8) Always conduct your searches in the same manner, so you don't miss any areas where a weapon may be hidden.

Answer key for Self Test - Use of Force

1. False
2. False
3. False
4. True
5. False
6. True
7. True
8. False
9. False
10. False
11. True
12. True
13. False
14. False
15. False
16. False
17. False
18. False
19. True
20. False

21. c
22. a
23. b
24. When you or someone else is in danger of serious bodily injury
25. b
26. open and closed
27. weapon's, reaction and straight strikes
28. weapon's, reaction, straight, two-hand lateral and rapid reaction
29. to the sky, to the ground and a rapid reaction strike
30. a
31. a
32. a
33. weapon's side or strong side
34. b
35. officer's name to whom you provided the information regarding number and location of strikes

Answer key for Self Test - Defense Sprays

36. A
37. B
38. B
39. C
40. A
41. A
42. B
43. B
44. A
45. B
46. B
47. B
48. C
49. A
50. B
51. A
52. B
53. B

Timothy Hightshoe:

Front Range International Defensive Pistol Association (IDPA) President // Safety Officer and Match Conduct Instructor // Peace Officer Standards and Training Board (P.O.S.T.) Certified Handgun Instructor // USAF (Colorado Air National Guard) Combat Arms Instructor // Defensive Handgun, Long gun Training Association (DeHLTA) Co-founder and Rifle/Pistol/Shotgun Instructor // Aurora Community College P.O.S.T. Handgun At-Will Instructor // Graduated from Denny Chalker's (Command Master Chief, Ret., SEAL Team 6) Executive Protection (knife/hand/gun) Training // Graduated Gun Sight Pistol/Carbine/Shotgun training // Completed Matt Burkett's Practical Hand Gunning course. // Veteran of Desert Storm / Desert Shield / Noble Eagle // Trained troops for Operations Just Cause / Enduring Freedom / Iraqi Freedom.

22966200R00043

Printed in Great Britain
by Amazon